HARE-RAISING Digest

presents

The Commons

WATERHARE
PRESS

THE COMMONS
HARE-RAISING DIGEST
A WATERHARE PRESS BOOK
ISBN: 978-1-99993112-1-6

Hare-Raising Digest copyright © Waterhare Press 2019

Cover Artwork copyright © Andrew Martin 2019

The Authors of this collection hold the sole copyright of their individual Works, and retain all rights to the Works except for those expressly granted to Waterhare Press for publication in this Anthology. The rights to Hare-Raising Digest and The Commons as a collective work are owned by Waterhare Press.

First Edition: 16 August 2019

Edited by Thom Boulton
Edited by Joanna Morgan

Waterhare Press recognises Sam Richards and William Telford as creative consultants on the creation of this anthology.

The artwork featured in the Waterhare Press logo is copyright © Pam Richards 2019

Waterhare Press is based in Plymouth, UK
waterharepress@publicist.com

A deviation from the social norm. A variance with the ruling ideology. Life. Love. Challenging tradition. Basic values. The right to thrive and not just survive. Human. Rebelling. Music. Change. Against the mainstream. Protest. Peace and prosperity. To be different. Counter corruption. Transition. Transcendence. Fuck war. Shun inequality. Attitude. Behaviour. Art. Philosophy. Morality. Health. Identity. Pride. Civil Rights. Aspirations. Beat. Punk. New. Better. Innovation. Utopia. Literature. Conversation. Politics. Existentialism. Mysticism. Spirituality. Defiance. Community. Sex. Drugs. Speech. Environmentalism. Radio.

HISTORY page 8
John Phillips

The Disposables page 9
Maryam El-Shall

Six Minutes page 10
Julian Isaacs

The Bookseller's Ocean Waves Goodbye page 11
Julian Isaacs

The Wages Of Reason page 12
Estel Masangkay

A Place At The Table/If You Have No Soul page 13
Linda Crate

Dead Letter Box page 15
Tony Noon

Deleted Tweets page 16
Hannah Linden

Black Woman page 18
Merris Longstaff

What A Witness Saw page 20
Tim Jones

A Harsh Remembering page 21
Gill McEvoy

The Arc Of Modern Political Thought   page 22
Ian Badcoe

Two Negatives Are Not Always Positive   page 26
Andrew C. Brown

It Is Always Who You Know   page 27
Andrew C. Brown

Angry Skies   page 28
Sarah Adams

This Is Not A Suicide Note   page 30
Hel Bee

Drapes   page 33
Mandy Macdonald

Silent Witness   page 34
Roz Weaver

Decades   page 35
Niall McDevitt

Bartleby In The Dragon's Den   page 40
Norman Jope

Melt Up   page 41
Eileen R. Taibos

Coming To Realise   page 43
Steve Spence

LINE — page 45
John Phillips

O Goddess — page 46
Thom Boulton

Hopeful/Hope — page 51
Kat Savage

If We Were — page 57
Hannah Linden

Concrete Pavements & Magnetic Doors — page 60
Abdul-Ahad Patel

Comes A Time — page 63
Richard Hillesley

Let Us Do Better — page 65
Linda Crate

Consensus — page 66
Brenda Read-Brown

Passing Into Legend — page 68
Steve Spence

SENSE   page 70
John Phillips

The Commons Manifesto   page 71
Sam Richards

Sing Me a Song of Freedom   page 80
Sam Richards

Song to Perfidious Albion   page 83
Sam Richards

Contributor's Biographies   page 89

HISTORY

The innocent confessed
their guilt.

The guilty judged them.

The work went well.

John Phillips

The Disposables

Return those broken things
That are not wanted
That cannot be used
That simply will not do.

Bruised fruits
And frayed shirts
And scuffed shoes
And darkened meat.

The trash heap is mighty high
The prisons are overcrowded
The rivers flow with poison.

Lonely souls wander the earth
Looking for a home.

Maryam El-Shall

Six Minutes

Due to the cold war
warming up once again,
The sun only shone in Moscow
for six minutes this month.
In the time it took to soft boil two eggs,
twenty-three people fell in love,
a silenced poet found the page,
And a lunatic rolled over
under ultraviolet rays,
refusing to die.

Julian Isaacs

The Bookseller's Ocean Waves Goodbye

ever since the clocks turned back
that little heartache in history
a rocket has not belonged in a sandwich
though stitching chapbooks to a train increases diversity

oral therapy is crumpled under the pages
of just one second hand book
every shade of psychology happens
underneath that shiny cover

the plum-coloured precipice of depression
means we deconstruct everything we see
in a kitchen aliens and pirates cradle dead octopuses
in a treasure trove as fast as a hat

due to the American government's ineptitude
on the steaming yellow sidewalks that hot day in New York
only one manuscript unfolds
into the expensive story of silence

Julian Isaacs

The Wages of Reason

to drift into the cycle of things
to accept the wages of reason
to allow blindness to make the most of mystery
 is living's most violent treason

to let you sway by sticks and stories
a double shame if by words
cover your ears and grapple the sword
unmask your piteous lords

if blood from your hands run down with your tears
let them go, if they with your questions
have provoked the wrath and indignation and fear
of men's greatest illusions

sing the song of the free,
or the shout of the rebel
the outcast who has asked some questions
turn them over in your mind or turn your mind over
before swallowing the lies of reason.

Estel Masangkay

A Place At The Table/If You Have No Soul

I

i'd rather die standing
than live on my
knees,
and i won't kneel before any
false prophet or god;
won't worship nor praise
idols
that i am meant to adore—
in the end we're all human
worthy of respect and love,
and we all bleed the same blood;
i won't put anyone on a pedestal
nor hold them in higher esteem
than anyone else
because when you cut straight through
the bone we're all fragmented souls
sewn together with the fibers of love
and stardust—
we are zillions of galaxies
rehomed and renamed from our original forms,
but each of us is beautiful and glorious;
we all have a purpose and a place at the table
i won't listen to anyone who says otherwise.

II

we need a better future,
i hope we can turn things around;
greed isn't need and people
deserve to be loved,
not things—
we need to do better for the environment,
and we need to preserve the land
before it is too late;
we need to reverse the curse
that is known as money
because once dead it can buy us nothing—
i tire of the corruption, i tire of the cruelty for one's fellow man
because if you cut to the marrow we're all the same;
and there's no reason to put anyone on a pedestal
nor to step on the faces of the downtrodden and poor pushing them
further into a state of despair—
we're all people, we all have hopes and we all have dreams;
one day i hope we're all recognized as worthy
because might doesn't make right and wealth means
nothing if you have no soul.

Linda M. Crate

Dead Letter Box

In this old trunk
are oranges, lemons
and that is all.
There were more
but I don't know
where we left them.

Don't phone me
with the answer.
Don't email, for sure.
Someone has the chopper
and they're waiting.

Tony Noon

Deleted Tweets

There's a god in me somewhere
if only I could find the switch to turn it on.

If I knew the right words I could order myself
to include everything I know about not taking time
by the roundabout.

Omnipotence is overrated when the variables
include mass level extinctions.

I should have realised the flood was a metaphor.

There's only so much you can fit into a bird's way
of looking at things.

Is this loneliness my way of not getting hurt
or just the way things aren't working round here?

Surely your inner god would have noticed
mine hadn't been around lately?

I've taken immodest leaps of faith but they never
take us the full journey across the canyon.

I'm making this up as I go along and no one
has had the courage to tell me I've failed.

There's a massive oil leak the size of a country
but they're still letting me pilot the planes.

I don't know how much clearer I could be
that I need help. That I can't turn my god on.

Without it, this is exactly what it looks like.

Hannah Linden

Black Woman

Black woman, black woman
Wat it is about har
Dat shi always in a war?
De war gwaan lang yu si
Anit ago somting like dis :-
Mi ear talk seh black woman too proud
Som no like how shi loud
Lazy
Crazy
Har hips too tick
An shi cyan lov a dick
Shi real sly
Neva cry
Ana shi cyan lie!
Shi too vex
Too camplex fi badda wit
Yu ear it?
Aggressive
Sensitive
All dangeras!
Mi serias
DAM
Som evan questian if shia real yuman

HECK!
A mistiak dem amek
It seem dem no kno
Black woman,
Is master chamelian wit tree yiy
De extra one give har access to the minds of dose who
dispise, lies and cries for har blood
With no sense of sisterhood

Black woman spirit pattern an feed
On harts, teers, sweat an blood of har ancestars
Dis harmi now fuse in har bone marro
Mek me tell unu someting fi true
Har army not happy
An dem no langa fraid of wat man cyan do.
Afterall, nyame war caan win and saive smaddy
From the rage of black woman duppy

Wen people anastan all dis,
Unu wud tink is comman sense
Fi mek sure,
Dem neva, eva, EVA FUCK wit a black woman
Unless, of course, dem waan si deman.

Merris Longstaff

What a Witness Saw

They squeezed on the boat
like the trucks they sent to Auschwitz.
Five to one square metre.
All they could do was try to cling
on what they found to hold.
It took us a year
to clear the remains.
No need for a camera.
The pictures for ever
scorched on my retina.
They went down together,
babies and mothers.
The toughest of workers
won't peel them apart.

Tim Jones

A Harsh Remembering

Not the *Harbingers of Spring*
but January's signature,
cold and long.

Unvisited by moth or bee,
their utter white
not virginal
but bleak sterility.

By March the snowdrops line the verge
like so much tarnished snow,
shreds of tattered grey –
again that surge of rage

at life so bluntly cast aside.
Round your broken body
snowdrops, frozen,
stony-eyed.

Gill McEvoy

The Arc of Modern Political Thought

I – Do not confuse me with a fellow traveller...

...do not make that mistake
I won't be manning any barricade
or spray-painting your slogans
on unattended walls. I am not breathless

for the state to fall. Evolution
trumps revolution, ninety-nine
point nine percent of the time
and for the other fractional percent: well...

we're so screwed anyway. Rebellion serves
only rebels, who—great though they are
at stealing jeeps, and wiring parcels
to explode—are not so hot in power

distribution, at bringing people light;
or heady freedom for the sewage
to flow in drains... no, theirs are not the brains
for that, for careful use of power

and fuse—how can they be? They need believe
such silly things along their way
such as *all men are equal,*
only our stance is doctrinally robust,

or even...
that they must prefer the electrodes
inserted here and here
to any tea-and-biscuit chat today.

II – Media rhymes with "eediot"

You do not understand the world
and let me make it clear
that this is you, you with the "Press" card in your hat,
who understands so very well

the breaking of a story like
a wave of noxious fluid
through everybody's living room,
it's you who just doesn't get it.

The world is not the news,
the dead are dead without your stare,
the bereaved still sad; and when
El Presidente bravely takes the town

from behind and rebels are all rounded up
I will admit you stop atrocities
for just so long as you look that way
and don't run off to the human interest piece

about the dog that saved the boy.
And I'm sure you say: *we give the people
exactly what they want,* to which I say
oh yes, you spin a world for those whose minds

don't let them find their own, and every word
implies what you narrate is what matters,
and what you don't ain't real. You'll claim
you don't conceal but every day

your untidy desk selects what's best for "news",
for folk to know: it's in the *public interest,*
you insist, while typing quote marks around
what the TV said the radio said
       about the other paper's views.

III – A plague on both your second houses

The problem is belief. Belief is stupid.
Belief it is that makes you make mistakes
and then it takes your errors,
brands them *heroic victories*

and makes you make them all over again.
If there is one thing that I know,
it's the stupidity of me.
I know, my brain is wired with

its tiny neural liars and systems
which conspire to enact a holy fool.
Cognitive bias, it does what it says
right there upon the tin, and which

you did not read,
because the idea was uncomfortable
but all you with the one coloured shirts
are *committed to your ideals*, which makes shits

of them there in the other coloured shirts
and all of you line up to grasp
opposite ends of one long rope
and grunt and pull and hope

to shift it just one inch
in your preferred direction
and you monopolise attention
for you, and your rope, and how

the other bloke is pulling the wrong way
while all around the horizon—boundless
and magnificent and essentially free—
stretches toward infinity,

but we're not allowed to look,
or speak, on that.

Ian Badcoe

Two Negatives Are Not Always Positive

political martyrs cry in anger from history
as families suffer loss for philosophical gain;
lessons leased by trust unlearned by community
allow unchallenged dictators to send us all insane

Andy Brown

It Is Always Who You Know...

Flimsy contradictions mask reality
images film disruptive community

cameras roll fumble focus towards
corporate pretence treading boards

(thespian deniers acting scripts
promising truth dead in crypts)

interring truth, greedy one percent
never explain where equality went

Andy Brown

Angry Skies

As the neighbours burned in the rain,
We had a nice hot bath.
They had
Desperate hosepipe showers-
Just over there, see them?
We fired up the Nespresso,
Dithered over elderflower and lime
Sugar free seedless organic
Or very-berry luxury conserve,
Croissants or cornflakes.

Radio on, and those neighbours
Drift in on the airwaves,
A global distance between us all
In a small kitchen-sized space.
We had traditional toothpaste cap
And too many dirty teaspoon debates:
Those pesky neighbours
Crept into rubble lined corners,
Craved invisibility,
While their babies choked
On foreign objects
Delivered from on high.

We choked too,
On unspoken dog walk turn resentments,
Coke Zero or Pepsi Max,
And wish you wouldn't do THAT...

After nextdoor's radio update,
The thought for the day:
' Thy neighbour or thyself? '
I choose my favourite tea,
We walk your favourite beach,
Stroke the dog, phone Mum.
Nextdoor seems less annoying.
We sign petitions, send some money.

Hoping to soothe
All our angry skies.

Sarah Adams

Not a Suicide Note

This is not a suicide note,
Though perhaps it should be.
It's just when I try to talk
About the pain and the hurt
And the void that drains
Life and light and joy
From the world I see,
I just can't do it.
Not in a way that makes me seem sane,
Just a normal person
Going through a bad patch.
Because I'm not. See
I'm different inside.

If the brain is a computer
It's fairly obvious that
Mine is stuck in a loop
Of blue screens of death
And reboots in safe mode.
But we are not machines,
You can't just switch me off
And switch me back on again.
Life just doesn't work that way.

Because,

This is not a suicide note,
And I refuse to be quiet.

This is my soapbox and I speak
About truths, that those who rule us
Would rather not hear.
This illness is no less real
For being in my mind.
It does not mean I'm weak,
Or I've been strong for too long.
You refuse to see how we suffer,
Brushing off pain with empty words
And dead eyed smiles.
Claiming to hear us, but all the while
Cutting back funding, and gutting
Services we need to survive,
All under the guise of efficiency savings.
To you I raise a two fingered salute.

Because,

This is not a suicide note.
It's a letter of hope,
That things can get better
And people will change,
And neuro divergence becomes a phrase
That rolls off the tongue
Without seeming strange.
And normal doesn't mean,
Not broken.
Because, I do not need to be fixed.
I am actual and whole,
I am a person.

Because,
This is not a suicide note,
I am still here.

Hel Bee

Drapes

liberty's sale in
a destroying
january
curtain department
    unsell
    able patterns
fawning
attendant
    lovely pattern innit love
ly pinkybrownygrey
    autumn mush
    room it's called
do you see the walls she says
yeah . i see them . i
see the bricks
faceless . hear them
rustling . maybe
growing

(& quite inviolable)

took a long time to build those walls
can you hear the bricks
crying?

Mandy Macdonald

Silent Witness

Today

I witnessed a man

headbutt a woman

in the middle of a busy city centre

as hundreds of commuters

walked straight past

pretending not to notice.

Today

I understood

how women are silenced

whilst she screams

at the top of her lungs.

Roz Weaver

DECADES
for the yellow precariat

∧

we have died for you oh masters
we have done our duty for you
we have done the right thing by you
our bodies and shadows as one
throughout the process we did not
connive with the wrong emotions
we know what to do with dross
we filled black sacks by the thousand
with dross (with us)
we did everything you asked nothing
of our own accord we ask nothing now
the days were dark as nights
but they are over we are faded
from the sphere that never fades

^
we have walked wheels of sun
and moon insentient in mornings
inanimate in evenings but obeying
the deep call too low to hear
wading through the fallout
of lies sins errors hates
the maps of guilt on which we fall
and fail our nations
with inferiorities and vices
too coded in DNA to atone for
the *grottes* we live in the *usines*
we work in deluged
we live and die in the flood
deaf but hearing the call

^
we have followed the courses of
your numbers your barometers
into the light and the cold
into the dark and the cold
we followed intense heats
solar depressions lunar depressions
lags of sleep to film it off
we followed the silences
we followed the insults
the inability to complain
to peaks to pits
work took us where it needed
places we'd not willingly go back to
places that don't remember us

^
the face of the dial was not ugly
as such not a human face
and if it seemed to smile at ten to two
or ten past ten the smile never lasted
the clock was the Form of the Good
and imitations hung on every wall
making us think in terms of hours
and minutes
that was a misprision!
the two hands were lifting lives
carrying them to crematoriums
if our Amazon wristbands ran out of charge
the invisible clock would not stop
to wait

^

thankfully the sound of time was muted
thankfully we'll hear the sound of time
no more

thank you oh masters

Niall McDevitt

BARTLEBY IN THE DRAGON'S DEN
for Mandy Burns

I stand before you, apostles of hard work,
hard profits and hard cheese…
but having no pitch, I yawn and cogitate
like Kaspar in the square with a letter
addressed to no-one and a gormless catchphrase.
So I shift from one foot to the other,
made clownish with cramp as the judges sneer.
'You don't have a plan, do you?'
says the one who's speaking for the ladder-climbers.
I prefer not to say 'I prefer not to say'.
Dismissed! Marched out of the camera's reach
to rot on a bench from the toenails up,
I must cling to time. For it is all I have.

Norman Jope

Melt Up!

I thought we would last
as long as the glaciers
of Montana, Greenland,
China, Norway, India—

We didn't last either—

But the story is bigger
than us: we decided not
to bring children to this
world of rising seas and
deteriorating ethics
among politicians growing
already fattened bellies—

But the demise of glaciers
create collateral damage
as far away as Borges' tropics—
reaching distances as far as
the span between gold and rust—

as far as the black dot
that, to us, was each other's
receding backs reaching
opposite horizons—how naïve

we were to think fate
is something we can control—

90% of human beings require
therapy and perhaps our
children would have survived
us to cure cancer, resuscitate

endangered species, or thin
those fat-bellied politicians—

If only we knew then
what we know now—

perhaps children, but
most certainly, we should

never shirk on love

Eileen R. Taibos

Coming to Realise

Did you know that Susie Quatro
is an Essex Girl? Ladybirds with
this infection may have a shorter

lifespan but even as a mod he
was a dandy of the east-end
streets. "Brexit has already

caused us significant financial
harm", she said. You may have
an awkward gait but this is our

secret bait for today and we need
all the time to be feeding. What's
wrong with America? "This is a film

about societal breakdown and
frenzy", she said. Is this a song
for Europe or a lament for a lost

world? Today we're going to meet
the swimmer who has just swum
around the coastline. This remains

a demographic with a poor sense
of entitlement yet there may be a
solution if we keep our nerve and

maintain the pressure. We owe it
to our audience to do more than go
on stage and regurgitate old songs.

Steve Spence

LINE

When we see a line of people the presumption is
they're waiting for something, & they know what.
It doesn't occur to us they might have no idea
what they're waiting for, or why so long in the rain.

John Phillips

O Goddess

She, Discordia,
where the head rests.

O goddess,
where we lay,
I examine every inch
of your bare frame.

Your mouth,
        angry, eating sacks of meat left for dead on
        slabs of grey bedding, so bony that nothing
        sustains your hunger, Discordia, brutal teeth
        capped gold
        crunching the gristle
        of unshaven unwashed unblessed meat,

Your eyes, Discordia,
        they give you away,
        one fixed on me begging to bring ecstasy, one eye
        veers right and clings to the poster of Enoch Powell
        defacing the bedroom wall,
        do you picture me as him Discordia?

The dimples in your back,
        where you fingered muscles for hours to relieve
        stresses,

       stresses you imposed on yourself,
       scars mark and damage your beautiful skin
       yet still you dig,

What about your tongue, Discordia?
       Split in twain like a two pronged fork, a carving fork
       stabbed in the side of any messianic torso that
       dares
       bare flesh,
       that dares to bleed red
       and not acid,

And your breasts
       heave and pause,
       choking lungs below sore nipples
       and grand mounds of fat,
       the smoker's cough is your ballad
       but you can no longer dance to it; no longer sing,
       your wheeze spits out curtains of vapour
       that mist up the windows,

Surgical cuts, faded indents around your navel,
       draw a map of ley lines, constant efforts to
       maintain cosmetic appeal
       has caused dead-tissue to sit below the hole where
       you were once fed,
       where you were linked to the Mother,

O Discordia, your judgmental vagina,
      wetted by pride, a traditional cervix,
      damn the cock cut or the cock drugged,
      it pisses on its intolerant throne
      made from china dolls and hate,
      so vain it will not suffer a mirror image,

And buttocks
      of steel
      and your coal coloured arsehole,
      shut tight to retain
      undigested beef cut in the bean field,

Your white palms,
      so greasy, so slippery,

           they forgot the black stains of the hilt from a whip,

           forgot the ashen blemishes made by passing a
           lighter over a quartz prism,
           blocking out spectrums of
           beauty, and gayness, and love,

           forgot the red and tan tinge left from pinching tea
           leaves off the Camellia,

           forgot the cinnamon smudges washed clean,

      forgot the coldness of peeling potato skins only to
      compost the de-eyed lumps in a bottomless pit,

O Discordia,
The scabs on your heel
      picked until hateful discolouration shows
      permanency,

The calluses of your feet
      stepping over the loose nails
      of the boundaries of our home,

The reek of fungus between your toes
      proves putrescent flesh is dominant,

All this forces me to dream of her,
I dream of Arcadia!

II

And how I do dream of Arcadia,
come, rescue me, Arcadia,
maiden of the green and great,

take me from the wretch,
love me and I will love you,
and our edenic offspring

will wail upon drifting free of your womb
and the cries will shatter the spines of books,
uncoil the spring,
and free every moment
to the unending pleasures we desire,

come rescue me, Arcadia,
from her.

Thom Boulton

Hopeful/Hope

Hopeful

I lie at the side of the road,
Limbs broken, heart cracked wide open,

Fried.

I watch the violence of the hopeless machine rush by,
I turn my gaze to the stars.
In the gutter of nature,
I can still hear the birds,

Grateful.

I feel real life slipping,
The 'sleeping ones', strip it slowly from my bones,
The Masters of false survival,
Rival of the richest-
Walk willingly into numbness.

I lie in the soft grass, just another crumpled outcome.
When time comes for me,
the ants, will be my witness,
the dew will wash,
the worms will feed,
the flies will come,
until once again, the earth will feel the sun where once I,
like all before me lay
(Nature knows how to renew her trash)

Peace

That I at least, may nourish in death, help flourish,
instead, of leaving a pool of human mess,

Care. less.
I lay wide awake, staring at the wild rush to nowhere,
Half the world in non-reaction,
Half in ab-reaction
A magnetic force attraction,

Yin
Yang.

Surrendering to this full world of pain, amongst the wild
grasses, I feel the purpose of my soul again;
my legacy is my true kindness.
(It's what we do with our little outcomes that count).

Renewed.

I reach out,
Drag my breaks and ruptures to the deeper grass. The
ghastly noise of ignorance quiet at last,
Away from tarmac, tyre and attack,
Away from break, crush, ignore,
crack.
I press my ear to the earth, the Mother sings,
We hurt together,
Everywhere,
Everywhere,

violently real,

Feel.

As I watch blind motion pass me by,
I cry my tears into the soil, make use of my gifts
I feed,
Whilst I can breathe,
I can seed.
I can be nourishment,
I can be need,
I embody all I have left to summon-

Hope.

I soak the earth and leave flowers In my wake,
They are barely seen, but they will grow tall,

Faith.

I start to flood the earth with tears- Something I can oversee, this tiny unseen part, I can rebirth.
Whilst I remain conscious and awake, this thought moves me.
Even with broken legs, I will stand for something,
I will stand for

Love,

With love, purpose, and with purpose,

Hope - a peace garden for the cracked and choked.

I have the power to heal things.

Belief.

I set my bones,
I Will this 'crushed spirit' away,

Sat in the grasses, I plant, dig, sing to the wounds,

Play.

I take a stand,
I find all I need in my heart,
I reach with my hands,
Until Help arrives,

Thrive.
We plant a new road,
We build the new way,
It will take time, with many breaks and sprains,
But what lays unseen,
Will have eyes on it once again.

Wide awake.

Whilst I live,
Wide awake,
Every beat,
Wide awake,

Whilst I have a wagging finger to point,
3 point back at me,

It starts here, this new world,

In our Hope of it,

Can you see?

Hope

I keep your four letters next to Love/Will/Dare and Free;
you devour Fear for me.

You are best friends with Faith and Belief,
you are the light at the end of Grief.

You are the dragging forward of my heavy burdens,
the rope climb through the uncertain,

and when I fall and drive my head into the sand,
you are the reason I can recoil and land.

I watch you whisper gently to broken hearts and fiercely
scream at pageant stars,

you twirl your embrace around everyone's dreams
(you are everywhere and nowhere for some it seems).

You swell when doubt creeps in,
you give fear a hearty grin -if miracles happen,
they begin with you.

You dare me to believe in more than I do.

You are the first and final feeling before any decision,
you break me out of my private prison.

Some assume you a delicate thing when
you're spoken,
a sort of fragile, emotional token,
but your serving power is beyond flesh and bone,
you are our original home,

a broken soul's rebirth,
The healing song of our dying earth.

You stand within the fabric of all being,
you are a Longing, a way of seeing,
driven like a stake into our hearts;
You are a bitter sweet and holy art.

You will define us all in the end.

How we choose to break or, with you, to bend.

It is in our failings that your truest form is revealed -
without you, none of our wounds would heal.

We are never left without
When we reach for you within,

In you we find love
and in love, we begin.

Kat Savage

If We Were

to think, really
think about it
we might want
to do something
something big enough
loud enough, bold
enough to stop
traffic, stop drivers
stop people, stop
people acting thoughtlessly.

At the base
of Life's pyramid
a third of
all insects threatened
with extinction. Birds,
big cats, primates,
lizards, whales, all
connected, all threatened.

Usually between one
and five annually,
extinctions now one-
ten thousand times
above normal rates.

If nothing changes
there will be

no insects left
by the end
of this century.

Do you feel
so worried now
that you feel
despair, hopelessness, dread?
Do you watch
the news, see
hurricanes, floods, famine
and think someone
somewhere, is doing
something about it?

Are you waiting
for big business
to be less
greedy? Less focused
on their stockholders
profit margins, their
jobs? Their stake
in keeping things
as they are?

Is it likely
they will save
the planet? Save
you, your children?
Your children's children?

If you were
to think, really
think about it
you might want
to do something.

Studies show that
twenty-five percent of
the population are
needed to change
the world. If
you can persuade
1 in 4
of your friends,
your family, people
you meet, there
will be change.

Don't despair: act.

Hannah Linden

CONCRETE PAVEMENTS & MAGNETIC DOORS

Concrete pavements and magnetic doors my morning starts on the sight of dawn
Persil bags tied to the inside of my trackie bottoms filled with rocks
9-5'ers on their way to enslavement but I have the audacity to glorify the trap
The trap isn't the risk, dangers or reputation. The Trap is the Elizabeth the second
Elizabeth the second that bounds my parents to modern day slavery in the form of a job
Chopping down sugar cane on the plantation was a job and life was payment
Not much has changed but the title of what we do
So, the trap allows Elizabeth to sit heavy in my pocket alongside the
destruction on my waistline

The fiends come out all day, but I avoid conversation because the horror of their lives will build more guilt challenging my vile justification
Chicken shop intervals, boss man always short changing me like I don't notice, but the beef isn't necessary because I don't yam pork
Fob hits the keypad, beep the entry releasing north from south. Would you believe the importance of science to a roadman of knowing magnetic laws; anxiety is released behind that heavy door.

Empty apartment, empty home, empty time, winter grazes my lonely skin, oven doors kept open to sweep the cold away. I take a break from the streets indulging in the strategies of 2K, precision in Modern Warfare and free running in Assassin's Creed.

Road life watching the 5-9ers return home, the traffic lights, car lights and bus stops show shades of the hell, but opportunity to others
BLACK male, wearing BLACK on BLACK, stop & search is instilled from school days as I'm institutionalised to a system that treats me like a slave
Click the teeth pass the handle as the cuffs squeeze onto my wrist, the same shackles that decayed on the wrist of my forefathers. Let it tighten, harness and bolt in immediacy. Let is rust through my BLACK skin, into my BLACK soul your repeated treatment is a mirror of history. I'm asked to turn the other cheek, but you have the cheek to label me BLACK. BLACK is the absence of colour; that is not my skin complexion so you can kiss my BLACK cheeks!

Concrete pavements, concrete grave is this where I'll lay one day?
Hidden under the drain I'm hopeful the sun in Africa will take me away from this islands grey clouds, I'm hopeful that although I'm bad mind there's a way out
Concrete slabs that hold the weight of the all black one tens, how many playful feet have you feature and how many more feet have you accompanied on those cold ice mornings and late night dwellings

See, your cracks begin to show, but I already knew they were there trying to attach to the other part of you that has broke because of this trapping nightmare
I'd fall between the gaps, but my ego is too big to let others see me vulnerable and although I crave the emotion of something that's taken by the dark and cold I can't let myself seem to go
Concrete Roads I'd follow your white lines to a new home, I'd run so freely that part of me will crumble until I reach that inner peace
I'd run so freely that all that is left of me is bare and barren and I'm reborn with another chance to be new

Abdul-Ahad Patel

Comes a Time

The sounds of the gutter were divine music to me.
I'd tune in two octaves below

and scratch the underbelly of the thing, stroking
my fiddle while the city burnt,

celebrating the colours, the maggots and the flames,
and the thrashing cacophony

of my audacious bow. I looked out at the world,
unable to touch,

and stood above the tracks fanning into the distance
like maps of ancient China,

the flash of a train rushing under the bridges,
yellow smudges of light

on the moving windows, motionless gulls high on the
river.
I walked the tracks

with a dim hunger inside me, and abandoned my dreams
to the ghosts of forgotten stairways

that reached from the riverside to the overhanging stars.
My heart was a bridge

to a distant shore. The smile behind my eyes lingered
far behind my eyes,

and I longed for that which I could not have, refusing
to know my place or ever touch the ground.

I raged at the cold summers and the turned up noses,
the Christmas days

and the melancholy autumns, and the ordinary mornings
unwrapping along the sky.

I longed for freedom to breathe and sang through the
gaps
in my teeth. There will come a time,

I would say, when my friends and accomplices,
the ne-er do wells and malcontents,

will descend in rags and put fire to the thing.
The mayhem is glorious.

The churches are burning. And the truth is at hand.
And the thing crawls along the edge of the sky,

and shakes its fist at me.

Richard Hillesley

Let Us Do Better

you let them swallow you whole: blood, bone, and marrow; you let them prey on your fears and keep your minds narrow—but i refuse these self-appointed monarchs and their self-appointed thrones, i refuse to listen to the lips of those who have never known of what they're speaking; who fight to oppress others simply to maintain a status quo—they expect the poor to carry the burden of the rich, but why should anyone be applauded for their greed or their cruelty? let the rich fall beneath the feet of all they've oppressed, i hope and i pray for a better world; where men are all truly equal and women are seen as equals not those to be subjugated beneath the thumb of man—i want a better universe than the broken spokes of this bicycle wheel hobbling around the sun mocking icarus and his wings when they wouldn't even dare to fly.

Linda M. Crate

Consensus

I once had a friend –
what sadder way can there be
to start a poem?
As if I had a friend, once;
just the one, and none now.
But I had a friend once,
who thought we could all find
consensus:
that the man too weary to buy
his third yacht
and the woman too tired to carry
water home from the well
could shake hands,
find common cause;
as if the town where every person
carries a gun, openly,
could be twinned with Totnes,
where you can try twenty-seven
types of yoga;
as if the couple on a farm
surrounded by wire fences
to keep out kangaroos
could adopt as their son
the professor whose studies are in
Sumerian dialects,
and expect him to take over
when they die.

We will all die –
those of us who want unity between countries,
and those proud nationalists;
those of us who welcome Starbucks
because they make good coffee,
and those who will not buy anything
from outside our own village;
those of us who seek consensus
and those who don't give a damn.
I had a friend, once,
who thought we could all find
consensus;
but we never really agreed about anything.

Brenda Read-Brown

Passing Into Legend

His appeal is real but it's visceral.
Are you going to let us operate
on him? "Like you I dabble", she

said. Negotiation should be a
continuous project but if you
don't think alabaster is sexy

you may need to check your pulse.
Are you an internationalist? Don't
worry about the smell, it's the colour

we're after. "Little and often", he said,
"little and often". If you are a master
glass-blower you are an important

person but trees that bend in the wind
survive while those that don't snap. Are
we talking about those blue remembered

hills or the green hills of France? Here
begins our scientific exploration of the
universe in earnest. How are we collec-

tively going to meet this massive demand
while also reducing emissions? "Jazz was a
form of symbolic resistance", he said. One

answer may be in the term 'collective' but it's hard to see the mechanics for change. "It's the next fish you've got to worry about", she said.

Steve Spence

SENSE

If we wait long enough,
it might well happen.

Then the wait — no matter
how long — would make sense.

If we wait a long while
and it doesn't happen

(no matter how long)

then the wait would
also make sense.

Only the sense made
would be different.

John Phillips

THE COMMONS MANIFESTO!

THE COMMONS is everyone, all of us.

THE COMMONS is a social, political
and cultural idea for the 21st century.

THE COMMONS is a political party
waiting to be formed.

THE COMMONS is a ginger group,
a way of thinking, a way of acting,
a big idea
and a way of being optimistic about the future.

THE COMMONS looks beyond
nationalism, scarcity, class division
and self interest.

THE COMMONS slogans are:
I BELONG TO THE COMMONS
 I AM THE COMMONS
WE ARE ALL THE COMMONS -
  suitable for T shirts, banners, badges and buttons.

BIG IDEAS

THE COMMONS is a core idea for today. It is a big idea. It is about who and what we are, how we relate to one another, to our own local spaces as well as the whole world both material and insubstantial, things and thoughts, In a world in which ecological and climate change are now more than mere threats, in which the nature and practice of democracy is under attack, in which desperately insular nationalisms spread like a virus and internationalism is unpopular (despite the fact that trade on all levels depends on it), in an age in which an expansive, humane view of ourselves is too often cajoled into narrowness of vision – in such a world we need a new core idea, a new story to tell about ourselves. We need this not only because it would encourage a better, fairer, more humane way of living. It is also about survival.

But what *is* a core idea?

Core ideas are ways in which societies may be understood. Victorian/Edwardian Britain, for example, was permeated by the idea of Imperialism. Much (but not all) about society at that time was related to this powerful idea. It was its major story about itself – or one of them. Or in the 1930s the American writer and historian James Truslow Adams coined the term "The American Dream" thus neatly naming an idea that already lay at the heart of American history and society. People still discuss it – for better or worse. In post Second World War Britain the big idea was Welfare – a benevolent state which cared for all combined with a post-war sense of starting again or rebuilding. Or there was the core idea of state communism which held sway in the old communist bloc. Since the 1980s the dominant idea in most Western democracies has been neoliberalism – the notion that society and economics should be based on as few controls as possible and that trade and monetary value should be left to find their own levels. Neoliberal thought has always held that an economy of this kind, which accepts that there will always be rich and poor, nevertheless has a "trickle down" effect that actually benefits everyone, the lower orders included.

There are always counter-currents to these big ideas. We should understand core ideas in nuanced ways rather than as simplistic formulae. And some of them are propped up by mechanisms which appear to contradict them. Neoliberalism, for example, has seen the growth of enormous amounts of bureaucracies and controls, the opposite of the "freedoms" it purports to celebrate.

You may like or dislike these ideas, but they all have (or had) widespread popular appeal. They may work well, if only for a while, but they all have (or had) real power. This power is always supported and spread by practices of ideology – in other words, by embedding the core idea in culture as expressed by popular culture, politics, education, the arts, particular views of history, and so on.

The encoding of ideas and ideologies is rarely simple or explicit. It is on more subtle, less obvious levels that ideology works at its most penetrating.

THE FAILURE OF NEOLIBERALISM

The 16th/17th century thinker Thomas Hobbes famously described human life as "nasty, brutish and short". Medical science and more enlightened ways of looking after ourselves have helped humans in the Western world to live, on average, a lot longer than in Hobbes' day. However, it could be argued that neoliberalism has encouraged the other two – nasty and brutish – in abundance. Whatever its merits and demerits neoliberalism is not a caring idea, and nor does it involve itself in things that can't be seen or measured. Improved medicine looks after our bodies, but our inner lives find no real nurturing in the neoliberal conception of human nature as essentially competitive and aggressive with the supposed law of the jungle now transplanted into urban settings. Neoliberalism is an extreme expression of social Darwinism's idea of the "survival of the fittest" – coined by Herbert Spencer, not Darwin himself, incidentally.

Industrial society, we now know, is the greatest cause of ecological change, seldom – if ever - for the good. Perhaps ignorance of this cause and effect was once an excuse. Yet although we now know how our actions affect the environment, still the industrial world's insensitivity continues largely unabated, a particular form of blindness which, of course, is ultimately related to the profit motive. Likewise the reason so little has been done to deal with climate change relates at root to an unwillingness to alter entrenched industrial practices which, of course, are also related to the profit motive.

This much is well-known. So too are many of the self-evident effects of a divided society typical of neoliberalism. We see them in the world around us. Divisions between rich and poor, on local, national and international levels are now deepening to alarming extents. Programmes of austerity by neoliberal governments hit the least well-off and most disadvantaged hardest of all. A significant contributor to these planet-threatening and socially divisive symptoms is the neoliberal tendency to monetarise nearly everything, to place business and the business model in pride of place, to implicitly encourage a kind of alienation from our world, our land, from others and even our selves. Vast numbers of people think and feel that it is time for a different idea, a different story to tell about ourselves from the one that neoliberalism implies.

THE COMMONS

THE COMMONS begins with historical facts. At one time significant amounts of land were held "in common". Nobody owned it exclusively although often enough local lords of the manor overlooked it. Local people had rights on the commons, and the commons themselves were used as gathering points. (1) The commons were also places where ceremonies and calendar customs were enacted and sports were played. Thus in various ways they were a focus of community solidarity.

It was not unusual, however, for the commons to be, in effect, stolen from the local people. From the time of James I to the First World War a total of 5,200 enclosure acts were passed in Parliament. The Enclosure Acts of the early 19th century had a particularly devastating social effect, especially on those rural people who were used to taking game from the land simply to feed their families. Suddenly this was made illegal and a poaching war followed. Thousands had to leave the land to find work in the new industrial areas. This was undoubtedly a deliberate effect of the Enclosure Acts: create – or make worse - rural poverty, drive people off the land, get them working in the mills, factories, and industrial concentrations. The people were robbed so that they could be exploited by the Industrial Revolution.

To use the idea of THE COMMONS therefore references the centuries-old idea of land belonging to everyone and to no one individual or interest. This history comes with its own warning about the forces that can attack the commons. It invokes tradition, but much thinking in more recent times has extended that tradition. For example, THE COMMONS can now refer to culture, the arts, education, health care, information and software. This last reminds us that there is now such a thing as digital commons – shared, free of access or open source. The traditional idea of commons calls to mind rural areas, but there is now discussion of urban commons whereby urban spaces and resources managed by local people or existing spaces are transformed into commons because of the way they are used.

The over-riding factor which unites all these different ideas of commons is that they are related first and foremost to usage and the generality of people. Their value has nothing to do with markets or market forces. Natural resources that we all need – fresh air, water, even the earth itself – should be conceived of as commons, as ours.

If the idea of THE COMMONS is extended in ways far beyond rural spaces and into all forms of 21st century life the implication is that user groups not only share and administer but actively participate. Therefore the idea of community is enshrined in THE COMMONS. As a term it encourages a communal, collective mentality. The Commons is not ruled by the market, nor by bureaucracy. A society in which THE COMMONS is the centre of gravity would not propose impractical decentralization, (which sounds good but is often unworkable in large societies) but perhaps a network of trusts, not unlike the NHS. Thus there is some centralisation where necessary, but not ruled by the state. Although it implies things held "in common" as opposed to privately, it does not necessarily rule out some private ownership. After all, when the pre-enclosed, pre-industrial commons in England were held "in common" there was also plenty of private wealth. They can run in parallel. If the land, or significant designated parts of it, were common there could be, for example, no fracking. "You can't frack on OUR land". (Yes, they do currently violate public land, but in a culture dominated by The Commons they wouldn't be able to...)

The social Darwinists (referred to earlier) created out of Charles Darwin's thought an apologetics for the idea that competition was fundamental not only to human nature but to the survival of all species. The Russian thinker Peter Kropotkin's book *Mutual Aid* redressed the balance and emphasized cooperation. As Kropotkin understood, we have the possibility for both competition and cooperation. Therefore a political idea based on the one does not exclude the other. However, as a sustainable survival idea a culture weighted vastly in favour of competition is not doing too well. THE COMMONS weights things in favour of cooperation and therefore tells a different story about ourselves.

THE COMMONS is all of us, not just those in a particular state, county or country. We are all commoners of the whole world. If we identify ourselves as such we turn away from the enfeebled nostalgia that today finds expression in nationalism, economic nationalism, putting our country first and having little concern with the rest. We become humane. In the global commons there are no foreigners, no migrants, and no one we wouldn't help if we could.

Like the commoners of old we assume certain rights, communal ownerships and responsibilities. We don't have to write or devise an elaborate political philosophy or blue print for society. That would probably be a disaster anyway. All we have to do is to understand and develop the habit of thinking in terms of THE COMMONS.

Sam Richards

(1) As in the village green of Tolpuddle where six Dorset labourers met in 1833 to form a Friendly Society of Agricultural Labourers, subsequently leading to their conviction for swearing a secret oath and transportation to Australia.

SING ME A SONG OF FREEDOM

Sing me a song of freedom,
The freedom that's ever in the wind –
Sometimes it's only a whisper illicit
Other times it's many thousand strong voices
That rise up and sing again.

Sing me a song of freedom,
The freedom to breathe without fear,
Where the roofs over our heads
Keep out the storm, the rain
And the terrors that keep us down
And grateful;
The freedom to be more than a number
Or a pair of hands
That someone you don't know pays for –
As little as they can get away with,
Freedom to sing in chorus
In the mountains and valleys
In the city streets, the rush hours,
By the rivers and tides
That flow and turn
As we watch and learn;
Freedom to be what we are
Not what we ought to be,
Ought to have,
Ought to spend,
Ought to ought to;
Freedom to know we're OK as we are

And don't you forget it.

Sing me a song of freedom
From round the world,
Freedom to call this the earth
That belongs to us,
All of us
In common,
And not to let them drill down into its veins
And scare it to death,
Or steal its diamonds
Or suck its oily blood
And pump it far and wide
Till there's none left.

Sing me a song of freedom,
The freedom to read the signs
From the heat of the sun
And the melting ice
And the freedom to deal with it
Before the unfree who listen to nothing
Sink us all.

Sing me a song of freedom,
The freedom to look at the stars
And play them
Like notes in the night sky
That choruses life and love

And all we hold in common
As neither commodity nor cost.
Sing me a song of freedom
For freedom makes us strong.

Sam Richards

SONG TO PERFIDIOUS ALBION

High on a hill and a little out of town with the moors behind and before, the merest breeze, and out there in front of our view in the distance is the city slung everywhere in the low land – suburbs, industry, inner and outer streets, downtown uptown, like a map of itself drawn over centuries, a picture without a frame –

Up where the songs of curlew and skylark drift on the wind and the lolloping landscape calls for an artist with time and colours – not a camera and least of all a phone – my years-back friend Carl and I say nothing but our thoughts follow our gaze, easy uneasy clear-eyed but interior, anxious at this crossroads of England's story hoping against hope that it won't let us down -

A view of the moment - it took no notice of us but just lay there in beautiful indifference clean and airy – and us wishing we were prophets of the new moon with wise words of reassurance for us for you for the many for the few –

With a slow sweep of his arm he took it all in – town country past present – and spoke of the world above, the mythic visible and invisible worlds of Anglia – the painful plough, the shepherd of the moors, Tolpuddle, empire and industry, dirty canals, poverty knock, Peterloo, milkmaids and highwaymen, Tommy always at war, suffragettes, factories and mills, steelmen, riveters, shipbuilders and ships a-sail, songs of the road from Stonehenge to call centres – histories of emancipation, histories of two solid feet standing alone for human rights, two joined hands – two four six a million –

And he turned to me and asked the question on both our minds: How did Albion become so perfidious? – and I thought of death and resurrection and wondered whether its magic could work this time –

We ruminated on lost ideals, on once-shining visions now disappointed and cancelled out by the noise of the rising right-wing, of demagogues of the gutter, cheap tyrants of the TV and YouTube peddling their prejudices as if they were something new, of the racist disease stalking there in the valley below and in the city where the cures are shoddy and peddled by inadequate cut-price Napoleons of a super-nationalist Hell right here – every damn thing we ever stood for now used as target practice for the slings and arrows of outrageous reaction and self-righteous indignation – and in our stomachs a dull dread of Albion as an open prison, a graveyard of liberty, a cesspit where nobler principles struggle for breath as they drown in belligerent unconscious inattentive deceptions where the people have spoken in a democratic haze –

How long can this go on, we asked aloud. How long? He grabbed a stone and threw it high, high in the air and we watched it rise and fall. We refused to accept that the fall was the end of the road.

For goodness sake, we declared to the horizon, let's turn our face to the sun, let's bloody well sing, let's dance, let's think – it's not hard to think, let's claim and reclaim, heed the wise and the opening of the eyes; you and I, we are not those festering apologies for end times served up as politics nor are we cowed into submission by the shabby mediocrity of their paranoid neurosis deluded into speaking one's mind as a form of ignorance; ("he speaks his mind" even though he hasn't got one and just shit comes out - rah rah for the disposable saviour, vote vote vote for your own subordination...); we're not that – we're the come-all-ye choruses of songs of generations, of spirit, of the days of ever; we are the rise-up-and-fight-again of the eternal drama, all of us, not just you and me - everyone -

We grasped firmly the historic urgency of the moment with the fearlessness of the fair, the determination to combine voices and sing in friendly unison; we honour the hedge priests of old, Lollards and lovers of the free, those who were thrown out or expelled, refusers accusers and confusers of the status quo, those who tell different stories and tell them well - solidarity, earthly angels who waged non-violence against the monoliths of power, those who started small and watched it grow –

We dig where we stand and this is our prayer – not to an absent entity but as determinations to ourselves:

We're not a down and divided threatened and wretched miserariat of the shadows who come out for a fight when the rabble rousers command; they have their story (if they know it), we have ours (and we should know it) – John Ball, Winstanley and the Diggers, Godwin, Shelley, Mary Wolstonecraft, the Pankhursts; but we also have minds of today planted back then but that think around the corners of tomorrow and refuse to salute palaces, citadels and institutions - we sing songs for hunting every new cutty wren, to welcome in the May and the new order, the New Year and farewell to the old; no gurus, no religion, no sacred books, no phony nationhood, no fatuous flag to flap in the flimflam winds of no change therefore getting worse –

Each of us is a new story in the telling - Carl, me, you, each an Odyssey unfolding, an enchanted Garden of Earthly Delights, an Eroica and an Ode to Joy, an outraged roar against war, a Song of Songs erotic and perfect – each of us has their story but our identities are in our souls that never do what they're told and never tell what they do, you just have to watch them -

And you, landscape of the moors and city, you are not ours although we love you from high up here on the moorland hill; you are yours and we are ours - our darkest hours come when we mix up the two - control possession ownership power over places and people, over difference unfamiliar and new – but we can, we will, we do claim all that has gone before, reinvent it, write it anew, give it voice, but not as slaves or masters – but as discerning fresh air alchemy, respectful visitors, people of the commons sharing loving uphill way down you me managing but not controlling out in the open all together in this precious space granite and concrete sheep and the railway so be it so be it...

Sam Richards

Poets
in order.

John Phillips
John Phillips was born in St. Ives, Cornwall and lives in Slovenia. He is the author of Shape of Faith (Shearsman Books, 2017), Heretic (Longhouse, 2016), What Shape Sound (Skysill Press, 2011) and Language Is (Sardines Press, 2005). His work has appeared in the following anthologies: From Hepworth's Garden Out (Shearsman Books, 2010), Haiku in English: The First Hundred Years (W. W. Norton & Company, 2013), Succinct: The Broadstone Anthology of Short Poems (Broadstone Books, 2013), Wave Hub: New Poetry from Cornwall (Francis Boutle, 2014) and NOON: An Anthology of Short Poems (Isobar Press, 2019).

Maryam El-Shall
Maryam El-Shall holds an MA in English and a PhD in Comparative Literature. She lives and works in Florida.

Julian Isaacs
Julian Isaacs has been writing and performing poetry since the early 1970s, when he first sold his work in pamphlet form in the corridors of Kensington Market. Also known as Auntie Pus (The Punk Balladeer) and citing his major influences as Michael Horovitz's *'Children of Albion'* and the Beats, Julian's poetry takes the listener or reader down an intense, and sometimes dense, eclectic lexical journey. He has recently had poems published in *The Broadsheet, Plymouth Herald, Spilling Cocoa Over Martin Amis, Poems Against Prejudice, I Am Not A Silent Poet* and *Razz*.

Estel Masangkay
Estel Grace Masangkay writes literary fiction and poetry. She currently leads a full-time team of researchers at New York-based startup AskWonder. Her favorite drink when writing is Hong Kong-style *naicha*.

Linda M. Crate
Linda M. Crate's works have been published in many magazines both online and in print. She has six published chapbooks A Mermaid Crashing Into Dawn (Fowlpox Press - June 2013), Less Than A Man (The Camel Saloon - January 2014), If Tomorrow Never Comes (Scars Publications, August 2016), My Wings Were Made to Fly (Flutter Press, September 2017), splintered with terror (Scars Publications, January 2018), more than bone music (Clare Songbirds Publishing House, March 2019), and one micro-chapbook Heaven Instead (Origami Poems Project, May 2018). She is also the author of the novel Phoenix Tears (Czykmate Books, June 2018).

Tony Noon
Tony Noon - Lives in Mexborough , South Yorkshire. Poems have appeared widely in anthologies , magazines including Acumen and Envoi , and local and national press.
Work can be found online at AllPoetry, Scriggler, The Camel Saloon and The Blue Hour.

Hannah Linden
Hannah Linden has many poems published online, in print magazines, and anthologies; most recently in Strix, Under the Radar; Magma; Proletarian Poetry; and the 84 anthology. In 2015, she and Gram Joel Davies won the Cheltenham Compound Poetry Competition for their jointly composed work, she was highly commended in the Prole Laureate Competition 2015 and

longlisted for the Rialto Nature Poetry Competition 2018. She is currently working on her first collection, Wolf Daughter, which explores the impact of parental suicide.

Merris Longstaff
Merris Longstaff was born in Jamaica, and emmigrated to the United Kingdom in the 1960's. Since then, she has worked consistently in the National Health Service specializing in Nursing and Therapeutic Counselling, whilst raising two children with her Cornish husband. As a descendant of the Windrush Generation, she has rich experience of both British and Caribbean cultures. Her work is written and usually delivered in an authentic Jamaican Patois style, which strives to tackle the highly sensitive subjects of racism and politics around the world with punch and humour.

Tim Jones
Tim is from the South of England. After a two year stint as a nurse in a local psychiatric hospital, he moved to the Midlands to work for forty years teaching Drama and English to sixth form students. After giving up teaching, he worked as an advisor in a referral centre and with other young people who have struggled in conventional education. As a writer, he tends to focus on radical political issues from Wat Tyler to Sylvia Pankhurst. His current projects are a play set in the 1974 miners' strike and a meandering sequence of unrhymed sonnets.

Gill McEvoy
Gill won the Michael Marks Award in 2015 for her pamphlet "The First Telling" (Happenstance Press). She is a Hawthornden Fellow; she used to run several regular poetry events in Chester but has now moved to Devon and is still 'finding her feet' there. Two full collections from Cinnamon Press.

Ian Badcoe
Ian Badcoe has been a scientist and engineer. His poetry explores themes of humanism, geekhood, gender, mental health, science, art, technology and literary genres such as SciFi and Crime. He has a long-term collaboration with German alternative rock musician Hallam London and they are working hard on releasing an album.

Andrew C Brown
Was 'The Grandad from Knowle West'. Recovering addict, ex-prisoner. Winner of community regeneration award. Achieved national Koestler Highly Commended Award. His poetry reflects life in and out of addiction. Two Crown Court trials; shared platform with serving Prime Minister; national, local radio; more than sixty poems published through three continents including The International Times; Magma; Ink Sweat Tears; and many anthologies. With heavy heart, dodgy hamstrings and realization of age, recently gave his cricket bat, pads and gloves to his grandson in the hope Harvey would make the most of any opportunity presented unlike his grandfather!

Sarah Adams
Sarah moved to Plymouth in 1983 to study Literature and Philosophy at Marjons. She wrote and produced a poetry booklet in the 1990s, and has had several pieces published in the Plymouth Herald. Sarah works with local charities to redistribute surplus food, drink, and toiletries etc. She is a musician and can often be found playing at camps, festivals and community music events with her partner John.

Hel Bee
Often poignant, sometimes angry, always personal, Hel Bee's poetry is her way to heal from past traumas and to find her way

back to herself. She invites you to walk with her awhile, under the light of the dark moon, and to listen to her stories.

Mandy Macdonald
Australian poet and musician Mandy Macdonald lives in Aberdeen, trying to make sense of the 21st and other centuries. After many years spent in working for human, labour and gender rights in British, EU and UN agencies, she came to poetry via Jo Bell's '52' project. Her work appears in print and online anthologies, journals and webzines such as *Songs for the Unsung* (Grey Hen, 2017), *Aiblins: New Scottish Political Poetry* (Luath, 2016), *The Poet's Republic,* and *I Am Not a Silent Poet*.

Roz Weaver
Roz is a spoken word performer and internationally published poet living in West Yorkshire. She has been published in a number of journals, zines and anthologies, including most recently with Snapdragon Journal, Voice of Eve and Dear Damsels. In 2018, her work was displayed at the annual Rape Crisis Conference, as well as being displayed and performed at two further exhibitions in London – 'The Sunlight Project' and 'Testimony', the latter as part of a conference hosted by UN Goodwill Ambassador Emma Watson. More recently, her work has been on exhibit with 'What You Saying?' and performed at Leeds International Festival.

Niall McDevitt
Irish poet Niall McDevitt lives in West London. He is the author of three critically acclaimed collections of poetry, *b/w* (Waterloo Press, 2010), *Porterloo* (International Times, 2013) and *Firing Slits: Jerusalem Colportage* (New River Press, 2016). He is a walking artist who specialises in the historic poets of London,

particularly Shakespeare/Blake/Rimbaud/Yeats. In 2013, he read at Yoko Ono's Meltdown in the *Future Exiles: Poetry and Activism* event. In 2016, he was invited to read his work in Iraq at the Babylon Festival. His book *BABYLON (a neoliberal theodicy) And Other Poems* is forthcoming from New River Press

Norman Jope
Norman Jope is the author of *For the Wedding-Guest* (Stride, 1997), *The Book of Bells and Candles* (Waterloo Press, 2009), *Dreams of the Caucasus* (Shearsman Books, 2010) and *Aphinar* (Waterloo Press, 2012). He has co-edited the anthology *In the Presence of Sharks: New Poetry from Plymouth* (Phlebas, 2006) and a *Critical Companion to Richard Berengarten* (Salt, 2011 and Shearsman, 2016). He also co-organises the Language Club, a live reading series based in Plymouth. A collection of poems and texts about Hungary in translation entitled *Gólyák és rétesek* (Storks and Strudels) has recently been published by FISz-Apokrif.

Eileen R. Tabios
Eileen R. Tabios has released collections of poetry, fiction, essays, and experimental biographies from publishers in nine countries and cyberspace. Her 2019 books include *The In(ter)vention of the Hay(na)ku: Selected Tercets (1996-2019)*, *THE GREAT AMERICAN NOVEL: Selected Visual Poetry (2001-2019)*, *Witness in a Convex Mirror*, and *EVOCARE: Selected Tankas*.

Steve Spence
Steve Spence is the co-organiser of the Plymouth Language Club, an organisation which puts on poetry readings at Plymouth's Athenaeum. He has published four collections of poetry, the first of which, *A Curious Shipwreck* (Shearsman, 2010), was shortlisted for the Forward Prize best first collection.

His most recent collection, *Many Red Fish*, was published early this year by Knives, Forks and Spoons Press. He appeared on BBC Radio 3's The Verb with Ian Macmillan in 2011. His reviews and poetry appear regularly in magazines such as Tears in the Fence, The Rialto, Litter and Molly Bloom. He recently read at London's Barbican Art Centre as part of a launch for The Long Poem Magazine.

Thom Boulton
Thom is the current Poet Laureate for the City of Plymouth. He is a regular performer in Plymouth and the surrounding area, reading at Cross Country Writers, Wonderzoo, Plymouth Language Club, and The Port Eliot Festival. He has been published in The Broadsheet, The Dawntreader, and Domestic Cherry, strange-poetry.com and uglywriters.com. Thom was involved in the artistic response to Poppies:Wave during its stay on Plymouth Hoe, and was featured on BBC Spotlight to showcase a robotics/poetry project with Volume AI. His debut collection Prima Materia was published 23rd November 2018.

Kat Savage
Kat is a singer songwriter by trade with a penchant for sassy quote writing and more recently, poetry. Passionate about all things mythical and magical, she spends a lot of time creating mystical beings to write about; much to the frustration of coffee shop owners around Cornwall. She writes under the name 'Fierce sister' from her home by the sea, which she shares with a mad dog, a house rabbit and a drummer.

Abdul-Ahad Patel
Abdul-Ahad Patel is a writer, actor and poet from East London. He covers topics from race, culture and religion which breaks stereotypes. Acting as an extended voice for the oppressed, forgotten and raising his voice for the youth.

Richard Hillesley
Richard Hillesley grew up in Kenya, South Shields and North Wales, and travelled widely through his twenties, working as a casual docker, book seller, railway guard, and yacht delivery crew, before becoming a computer programmer, and moving to Devon as feature writer and later editor of the first UK Linux magazine. Unbanging the Nails, a collection of his stories, is published by Clochoderick Press later this year

Brenda Read-Brown
In 2001, Brenda Read-Brown left a secure career in IT project management to be a fulltime poet and writer; it seemed a good idea at the time. Since then, she has won many poetry slams in the UK, and performs everywhere she can - Texas, Denmark, the middle of the Atlantic, the House of Lords, radio 4, many festivals, and quite a few low dives. Her first collection (2013) was Arbitrary edges, and in November 2018, V Press published a book of her page poetry, Like love. Her greatest joy comes from helping others find their words.

Sam Richards
Sam Richards is an improviser, composer, folklorist, poet and writer. He lectures part-time at the Academy of Music and Sound, Exeter, and lectured at Dartington College of Arts and Plymouth University. He lives in South Devon, although grew up in London. He has performed all over the UK, in France, Canada and the United States. His "About Time – Voices" was premiered in San Francisco by the Cornelius Cardew Choir (2009). He contributed many pieces to the Peninsula Arts annual contemporary music festival, notably *Kropotkin* (2009) which was performed by over 40 players spread throughout three floors and large ground area of Plymouth University's

Levinsky Building. His *Fish Music* in which fish in a large tank become musical notation was performed at the National Marine Aquarium, Plymouth, the Millennium Centre, Cardiff, and broadcast on BBC Radio 3.

His books include Sonic Harvest (1992), John Cage as… (1996), The Engaged Musician (2013), and Dartington College of Arts - Learning by Doing (2015).

Digest
Issue 1 team.

Chief Editor (development and selection)
Thom Boulton

First Editor (development)
Joanna Morgan

Second Editor (selection)
Sam Richards

Second Editor (selection)
William Telford

Cover Artist (development)
Andrew Martin

www.ingramcontent.com/pod-product-compliance
Lightning Source LLC
Chambersburg PA
CBHW061457040426
42450CB00008B/1400